I0430283

2011

The National Counterterrorism Center

★ REPORT ON TERRORISM

Information available as of March 12, 2012
was used for this report.

Office of the Director of National Intelligence
National Counterterrorism Center
Washington, DC 20511

Table of
CONTENTS

FORWARD › Developing Statistical Information

The National Counterterrorism Center (NCTC) was created in 2004 to ensure, in part, that U.S. government agencies have appropriate access to and receive the intelligence necessary to accomplish their assigned missions. NCTC is the U.S. government's central and shared knowledge bank on international terrorism and, in this capacity, NCTC provides the Department of State with statistical information to assist it in completing the annual *Country Reports on Terrorism* (CRT). NCTC also uses this information to compile its own annual *NCTC Report on Terrorism* (NRT).

Title 22, Section 2656f of the United States Code (U.S.C.) requires the Department of State to include in its annual report, "to the extent practicable, complete statistical information on the number of individuals, including United States citizens and dual nationals, killed, injured, or kidnapped by each terrorist group during the preceding calendar year." In compiling the figures of terrorist incidents that are included in the CRT and the NRT, NCTC uses the definition of terrorism found in Title 22, which provides that terrorism is "premeditated, politically motivated violence perpetrated against noncombatant targets by subnational groups or clandestine agents." (See, 22 U.S.C. § 2656f(d)[2]).

NCTC maintains its statistical information on the U.S. government's authoritative and unclassified database on terrorist acts, the Worldwide Incidents Tracking System (WITS). The primary function of WITS is to provide terrorism statistics to the Department of State for preparation of its annual report. WITS uses a well-defined methodology that involves documented coding practices for categorizing and enumerating relevant statistics. WITS is accessible on the NCTC Web site, www.nctc.gov, providing the public with a transparent view of the NCTC data. The data posted to the website is updated on a quarterly basis, pursuant to a rigorous 90-day review and vetting process.

The statistical material in this unclassified report is drawn from terrorism incidents that occurred in 2011, as reported in open source information. This open source material is the most comprehensive resource that NCTC can use to compile and provide the statistical data necessary to the Department of State to fulfill its legislative reporting requirements.

While open source material provides an unparalleled expanse of information, the credibility of sources may vary. For example, the ability of WITS to provide specific details on incident victims, the perpetrators responsible, or the extent of the damage incurred is limited by access to reliable open source reporting. Moreover, incidents that involve few casualties or occur in restricted or remote areas may appear in only a limited selection of open sources.

NCTC cautions against using attack data alone to determine the effectiveness of counterterrorism efforts to prevent incidents or reduce terrorist capacity. Counting protocols in sorting data are necessary but often require the subjective judgment of the person or agency compiling the data. For example, NCTC dictates that events identified as simultaneous and coordinated be recorded as one attack. As such, when over 15 attacks targeting three different cities took place in Nigeria between December 22 and 23, 2011, NCTC counted them as a single event because they were coordinated according to a central plan. Other counting protocols may register these attacks as 15 separate incidents. Additionally, annual comparisons of the total number of attacks alone do not measure terrorist threat for the basic reason that many attacks may cause little harm, while one single attack may harm many.

As such, this NRT is provided for general statistical purposes only. Observations made on this statistical material relating to the frequency, intensity, or nature of the incidents are offered only as part of the analytic work of NCTC and may not reflect the assessments of other U.S. government departments and agencies. Nothing in this report should be construed as a determination that individuals associated with incidents have been found guilty of terrorism or criminal offense.

The reader is encouraged to use this NRT as a guide to review publicly reported annual terrorist activity. Tracking terrorist incidents helps to understand important characteristics, patterns, and trends that surround terrorism, and helps to advance analysis and research. The ultimate goal in following incidents as they occur, however, is to maintain global awareness of the persistent threat terrorism poses and the critical need to secure its defeat.

National Counterterrorism Center

National Counterterrorism Center

The Methodology Used to Compile the WITS Database of Terrorist Incidents

WITS is the U.S. government's unclassified, authoritative database on terrorist incidents. Initiated in 2004, WITS collects data from a wide selection of international and domestic open sources and catalogs terrorist attacks into the database. This statistical information is posted onto NCTC's website on a quarterly basis for public view.

In order to track terrorism, a clear definition must be provided to ensure objective and consistent recording. WITS uses the U.S.C. definition of terrorism as the guiding mechanism for the database. Title 22, Section 2656f(d)[2] of the U.S.C. provides that terrorism is "premeditated, politically motivated violence perpetrated against noncombatant targets by subnational groups or clandestine agents." This U.S.C. definition of terrorism is the cornerstone of WITS data entry and an incident must meet the provided criteria to be entered into the database.

A methodology was established to systematically process the vast amount of open source information collected by WITS. From 2007 to 2009, annual methodology conferences comprised of analysts and academia were conducted as a rigorous exercise in collaboration and evaluation to establish sound counting rules and processes to collect and code information for WITS. The result of the collaboration was a methodology that permits both expansive searches and credible results.[1]

Terrorists, under the WITS methodology, must have initiated and executed an attack for the attack to be included in the database. Specifically, the incident must have resulted in some sort of active, kinetic effect–such as an explosion or inflicted injury or damage. Failed or foiled attacks, hoaxes, spontaneous hate crimes, and genocide are not included.

The WITS database contains over 85,000 incidents. More than 90 search fields are in the database to facilitate productive and independent searches by the user. Key fields, including "event," "victim," and "perpetrator types," provide details about the nature of cataloged terrorist incidents.

Event types cataloged in WITS include, but are not limited to, armed attack, kidnapping, bombing, and assault. Some coding is straight forward, other coding practices are more involved. For instance, incidents involving mortars, rockets, and rocket-propelled grenades are coded as armed attacks, not bombings, because they employ fired weapons. Attacks using improvised explosive devices (IED) and vehicle-borne IEDs (VBIED) are coded in a distinct category under bombing to indicate when altered, adapted, or homemade munitions were utilized. Information about suicide events is also captured.

Victim types cataloged in WITS include, but are not limited to, civilians, business people, students, military, and police. Victims' nationalities are also recorded in WITS where open source media reports such information. The methodology presumes most victims to be local nationals unless otherwise reported in the press.

Perpetrator information is included in WITS, but under select criteria. A group will be included in WITS only if it has been designated as a Foreign Terrorist Organization by the Department of State, if it has claimed status as a terrorist group or responsibility for terrorist acts, or if it has been repeatedly and reliably suspected of terrorist activity. When reporting provides detailed information, a confidence level as to the identity of the perpetrator of "likely," "plausible," or "unlikely" can be

---

1 NCTC does not conduct research other than a review of information contained in open source reporting. NCTC is not responsible for errors and omissions in open source reporting. The judgment of NCTC is not intended to be a legally binding determination that an event is a terrorist act, and is provided solely as statistical information.

cataloged. NCTC may also infer the identity of a perpetrator, when none is identified, in instances where only one group is active in the particular region in question or the various attack characteristics match the modus operandi of a single group.

In order to be more analytically useful, the database also provides specification with respect to the impact of attacks. For instance, killed, wounded, and kidnapped figures are provided with as much detail as possible. In addition, targeting characteristics are coded that register violence that appears to target certain groups, including cultural, ethnic, or religious groups. Where facilities have been attacked, damage estimates are listed as Light ($1 to $500 thousand), Moderate ($500 thousand to $20 million), or Heavy (over $20 million).

Determining when noncombatants have been targeted, as provided in the U.S.C. definition, can be challenging. NCTC developed a combatant matrix that details the various areas of war-like settings and the common combatant or combatant-like actors such as military police, militias, and soldiers. NCTC utilizes this combatant matrix to determine when an act targeting combatant-like actors should be included in WITS. To remain as accurate as possible, the combatant matrix is adjusted when circumstances surrounding world conflicts change.

In the cases of Iraq and Afghanistan, it can be difficult to gather comprehensive information about all attacks. For instance, distinguishing terrorism from other forms of violence, such as sectarian violence in Iraq, is usually complex. In addition, over the past year, there was a noted decline in open source reporting in Afghanistan. Due to these conditions, the WITS dataset likely undercounts the number of attacks in Iraq and Afghanistan for 2011.

It is important that readers of this report recognize that it is based on data collected through the distinct methodology employed by WITS. Other institutions and parties processing statistical terrorism data may employ methodologies that yield different results. In addition, while reviewing the NRT, readers are encouraged to study all statistical categories presented to gain a more balanced perspective on global terrorist events as they occurred. With that in mind, the statistical information provided in the NRT is a comprehensive source of information on terrorism incidents for 2011 and can serve as valuable reference.

National Counterterrorism Center

NCTC Observations on the Statistical Material Provided by WITS

Overarching Trends

Over 10,000 terrorist attacks occurred in 2011, affecting nearly 45,000 victims in 70 countries and resulting in over 12,500 deaths. The total number of worldwide attacks in 2011, however, dropped by almost 12 percent from 2010 and nearly 29 percent from 2007. Although the 2011 numbers represent five-year lows, they also underscore the human toll and geographic reach of terrorism. The Near East and South Asia continued to experience the most attacks, incurring just over 75 percent of the 2011 total. In addition, Africa and the Western Hemisphere experienced five-year highs in the number of attacks, exhibiting the constant evolution of the terrorist threat.

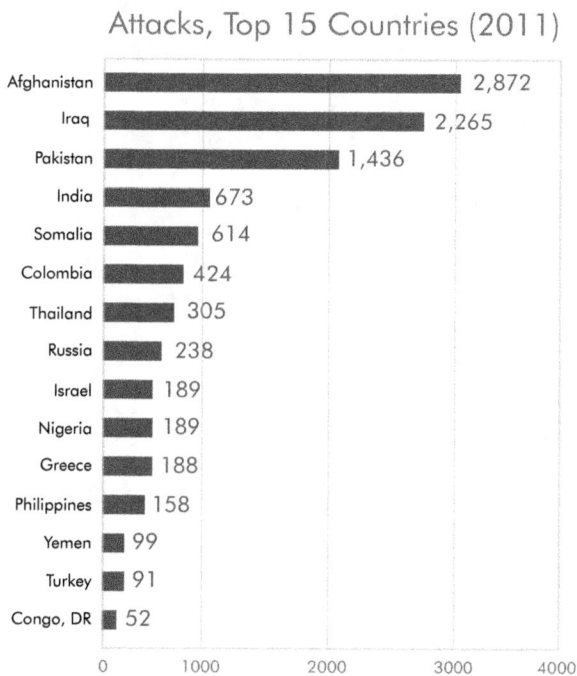

Attacks, Top 15 Countries (2011)

Country	Attacks
Afghanistan	2,872
Iraq	2,265
Pakistan	1,436
India	673
Somalia	614
Colombia	424
Thailand	305
Russia	238
Israel	189
Nigeria	189
Greece	188
Philippines	158
Yemen	99
Turkey	91
Congo, DR	52

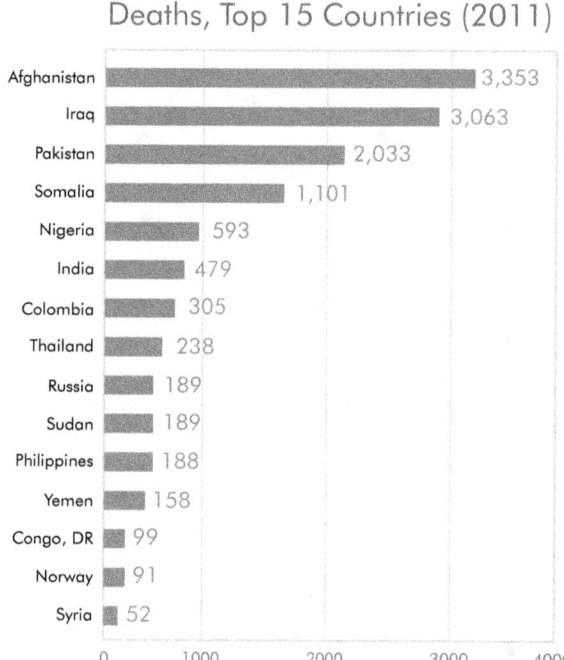

Deaths, Top 15 Countries (2011)

Afghanistan	3,353
Iraq	3,063
Pakistan	2,033
Somalia	1,101
Nigeria	593
India	479
Colombia	305
Thailand	238
Russia	189
Sudan	189
Philippines	188
Yemen	158
Congo, DR	99
Norway	91
Syria	52

- Africa experienced 978 attacks in 2011, an 11.5 percent increase over 2010. This is attributable in large part to the more aggressive attack tempo of the Nigeria-based terrorist group Boko Haram, which conducted 136 attacks in 2011—up from 31 in 2010.

- Attacks in Europe and Eurasia fell 20 percent from 703 in 2010 to 561 in 2011. The greatest decline occurred in Russia where terrorist attacks were down from 396 in 2010 to 238 in 2011. In contrast, Turkey experienced a spike in terrorist attacks, rising from 40 in 2010 to 91 in 2011. Together, Russia and Turkey suffered almost 70 percent of all 2011 terrorism-related deaths in Europe and Eurasia.

- Terrorist attacks in the Western Hemisphere rose nearly 40 percent from 343 in 2010 to 480 in 2011, the vast majority of which were ascribed to the Revolutionary Armed Forces of Colombia (FARC).

- The number of terrorist attacks in East Asia and the Pacific declined for the fifth consecutive year, falling 25 percent from 724 in 2010 to 543 in 2011, and 62 percent from the peak of 1,423 in 2007. Thailand and the Philippines continued to be the primary terrorist targets in the region.

- The Near East and South Asia suffered 7,721 attacks and 9,236 deaths. The majority of those occurred in just three countries—Afghanistan, Iraq, and Pakistan—which, together, accounted for 85 percent of attacks in these regions and almost 64 percent of attacks worldwide. While attacks in Afghanistan and Iraq decreased from 2010 by 14 and 16 percent, respectively, attacks in Pakistan increased by 8 percent.[1]

Trends in Iraq, Afghanistan, and Pakistan: Attacks & Deaths
2007-2011

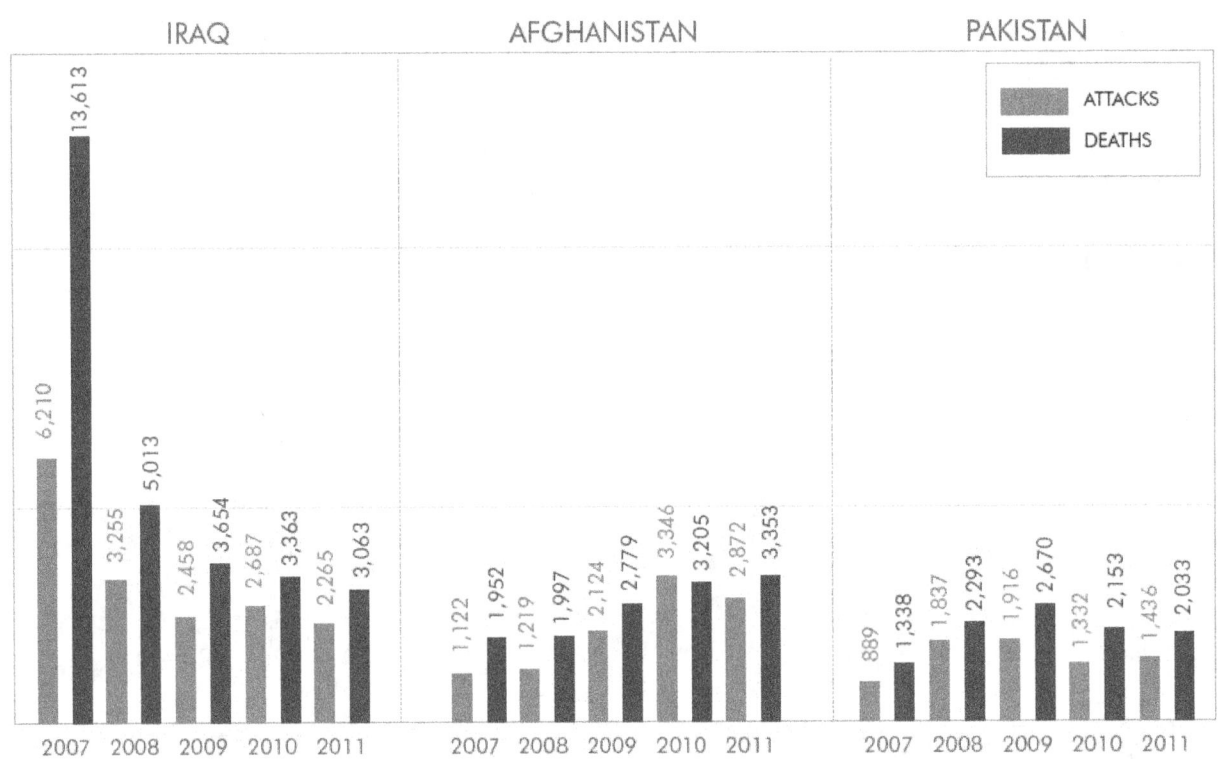

1 Trend analysis for Afghanistan includes inconsistent source reporting between 15 November and 31 December 2011.

Perpetrators

S unni extremists accounted for the greatest number of terrorist attacks and fatalities for the third consecutive year. More than 5,700 incidents were attributed to Sunni extremists, accounting for nearly 56 percent of all attacks and about 70 percent of all fatalities. Among this perpetrator group, al-Qa'ida (AQ) and its affiliates were responsible for at least 688 attacks that resulted in almost 2,000 deaths, while the Taliban in Afghanistan and Pakistan conducted over 800 attacks that resulted in nearly 1,900 deaths. Secular, political, and anarchist groups were the next largest category of perpetrators, conducting 2,283 attacks with 1,926 fatalities, a drop of 5 percent and 9 percent, respectively, from 2010.

- Attacks by AQ and its affiliates increased by 8 percent from 2010 to 2011. A significant increase in attacks by al-Shabaab, from 401 in 2010 to 544 in 2011, offset a sharp decline in attacks by al-Qa'ida in Iraq (AQI) and a smaller decline in attacks by al-Qa'ida in the Arabian Peninsula (AQAP) and al-Qa'ida in the Islamic Maghreb (AQIM).

- The most active of the secular, political, and anarchist groups in 2011 included the FARC (377 attacks), the Communist Party of India-Maoist (CPI-Maoist) (351 attacks), the New People's Army/Communist Party of the Philippines (NPA-CPP) (102 attacks), and the Kurdistan Worker's Party (PKK) in Turkey (48 attacks).

Deaths Grouped by Perpetrator Type (2011)

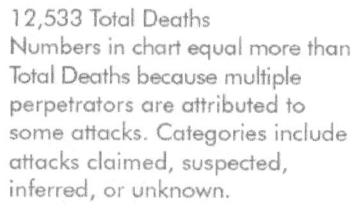

12,533 Total Deaths
Numbers in chart equal more than Total Deaths because multiple perpetrators are attributed to some attacks. Categories include attacks claimed, suspected, inferred, or unknown.

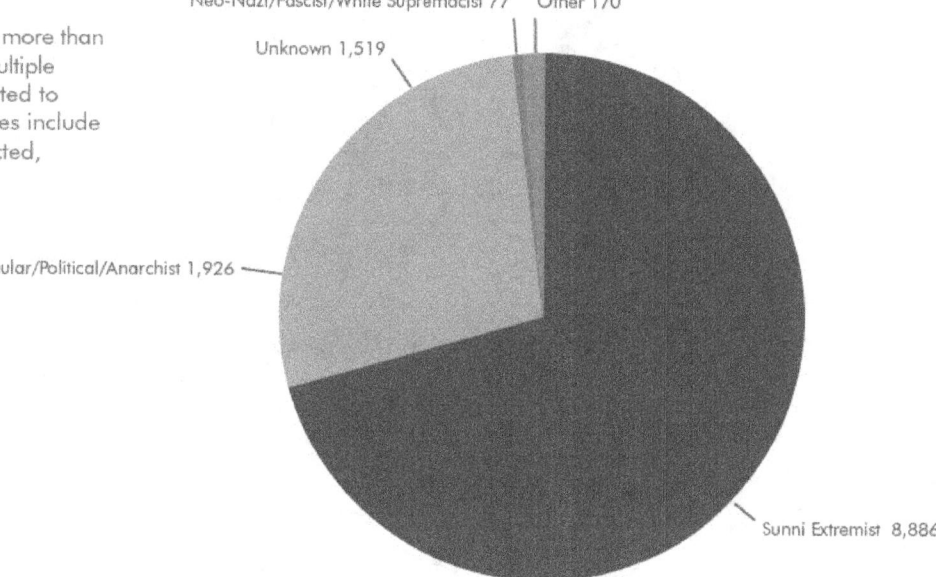

Neo-Nazi/Fascist/White Supremacist 77   Other 170

Unknown 1,519

Secular/Political/Anarchist 1,926

Sunni Extremist 8,886

Notable 2011 Sunni Extremist Attacks Cataloged in WITS:

- On June 3, in Sanaa, Yemen, suspected AQAP members bombed the Presidential Palace, injuring President Ali Abdallah Salih and Prime Minister Ali Muhammad Mujawar, and killing and injuring 16 members of their entourage and bodyguards. This was the only attack in 2011 where a sitting head of state was wounded.

- On August 26, in Abuja, Nigeria, Boko Haram conducted its first attack against a foreign target with a suicide Vehicle-Borne Improvised Explosive Device (VBIED) attack on the United Nations compound in Abuja, Nigeria, killing 12 UN staff members and 12 others and wounding 115 persons. This is the largest terrorist attack in the country to date.

- On September 20, in Kabul, Afghanistan, a suspected Taliban suicide bomber detonated an Improvised Explosive Device (IED) at the residence of the former President of Afghanistan and current Peace Council Chief, killing the Peace Council Chief and five others and wounding several civilians.

- On October 4, in Mogadishu, Somalia, a suspected al-Shabaab suicide bomber drove a truck into a government compound and detonated a VBIED, killing 91 civilians and nine children and wounding 164 civilians and children. This incident resulted in the most total victims of any single attack during 2011.

Other Notable Attacks Cataloged in WITS:

- On March 13, in Nzako, Central African Republic, suspected Lord's Resistance Army (LRA) assailants attacked the village, killing 12 civilians, kidnapping more than 100 others (including children) and setting fire to and looting the village.

- On July 22, in Oslo, Norway, a politically-motivated lone wolf first detonated a VBIED outside the Prime Minister's office, killing seven government employees and one civilian and wounding 30 other civilians. Two hours later, on Utoya Island, the same assailant then fired upon a Norwegian Labor Party-associated youth camp, killing 67 people and two police officers and injuring 66 others.

National Counterterrorism Center

Types of Attacks

Armed attacks and bombings constituted nearly 80 percent of all terrorist attacks in 2011. Suicide attacks accounted for just 2.7 percent of terrorist attacks last year but 21 percent of all terrorism-related fatalities, a fact that underscores their extreme lethality. IEDs were the most frequently used and deadliest terrorist weapon employed.

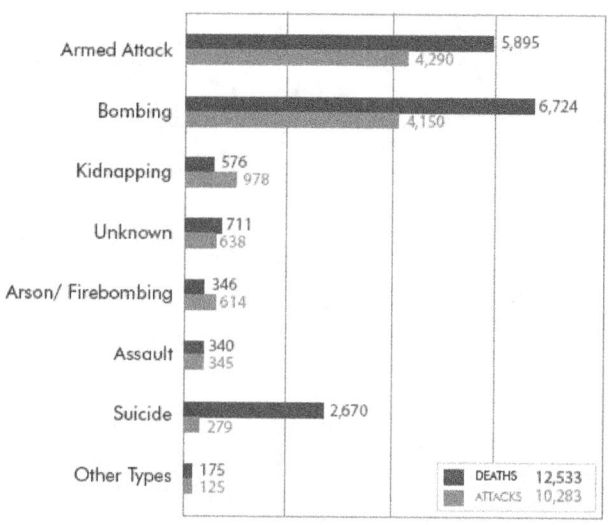

Number of Attacks and Deaths
by Attack Type (2011)

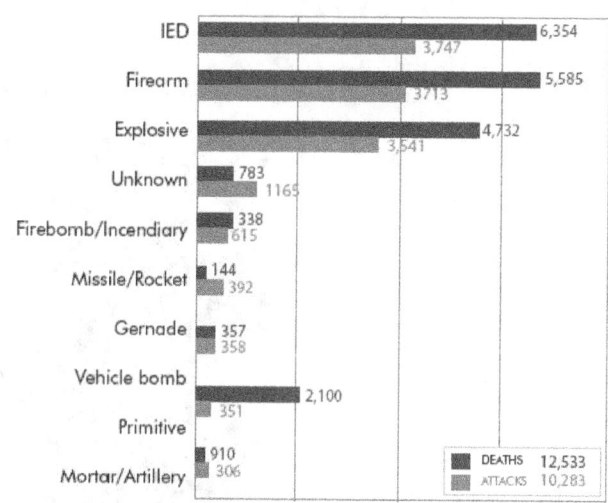

Number of Attacks and Deaths
by Weapon Type (2011)

- The number of bombings has remained relatively consistent over the past five years, ranging between approximately 4,000 and 4,500 annually. In contrast, the number of armed attacks has steadily decreased from a high of 7,958 in 2007 to 4,290 in 2011.

- Suicide attacks rose from 264 in 2010 to 279 in 2011. In spite of the increase, this represents a sharp drop from the five-year peak of 520 suicide attacks in 2007. Sunni extremists conducted 93 percent of suicide attacks.

- Terrorism-related kidnapping events and deaths, 978 and 576, respectively, hit five-year lows.

Kidnapping Victims, Top 15 Countries (2011)

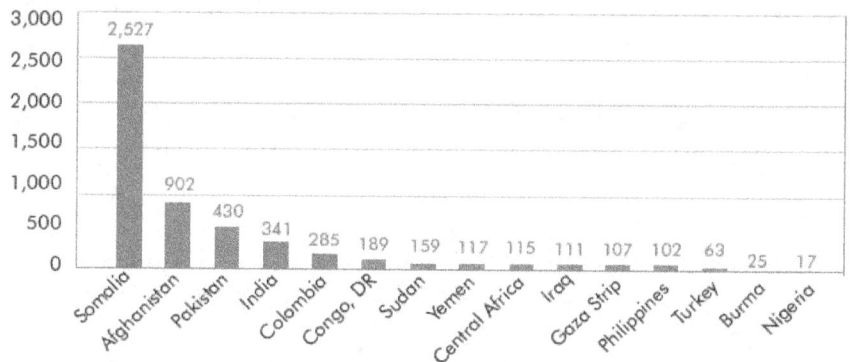

Victims of Attacks

O ver 12,000 people were killed by terrorist attacks in 2011. The overall number of victims killed, however, decreased 5 percent from 2010. More than half of the people killed in 2011 were civilians and 755 were children. Although terrorism deaths decreased, the number of government representative and security force fatalities increased significantly. Muslims continued to bear the brunt of terrorism, while attacks targeting Christians dropped nearly 45 percent from a five-year high in 2010.

Deaths by Victim Categories, Top Nine (2011)

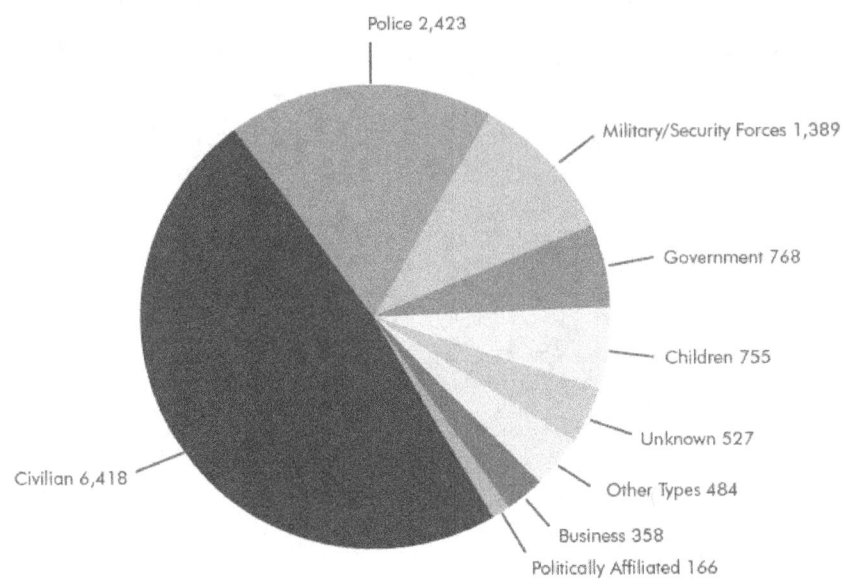

- Although civilians were the largest single group of victims killed in terrorist attacks, their numbers over the past five years in proportion to the total number of deaths have gone down by 13 percent, decreasing from a 2007 high of 64 percent.

- The number of government employees and contractors killed in 2011 increased by over 60 percent from 2010, while the number of government officials killed in 2011 increased by over 13 percent. The number of police killed in 2011 also increased by over 15 percent.

- In cases where the religious affiliation of terrorism casualties could be determined, Muslims suffered between 82 and 97 percent of terrorism-related fatalities over the past five years.

- Muslim majority countries bore the greatest number of attacks involving 10 or more deaths, with Afghanistan sustaining the highest number (47), followed by Iraq (44), Pakistan (37), Somalia (28), and Nigeria (12).

- Afghans also suffered the largest number of fatalities overall with 3,245 deaths, followed by Iraqis (2,958), Pakistanis (2,038), Somalis (1,013), and Nigerians (590).

National Counterterrorism Center ⎯⎯⎯

Attacks Against Facilities

O ver two-thirds of all terrorist attacks struck infrastructure or facilities. Of those, transportation assets and public places were the most frequently targeted. Transportation facilities—such as vehicles, buses, and transportation infrastructure—incurred damage in about 27 percent of the attacks, while public places—including communal areas, markets, polling stations, religious institutions, schools, and residences—incurred damage in about 21 percent of the attacks.

Attacks Damaging Facilities by Facility Category (2011)

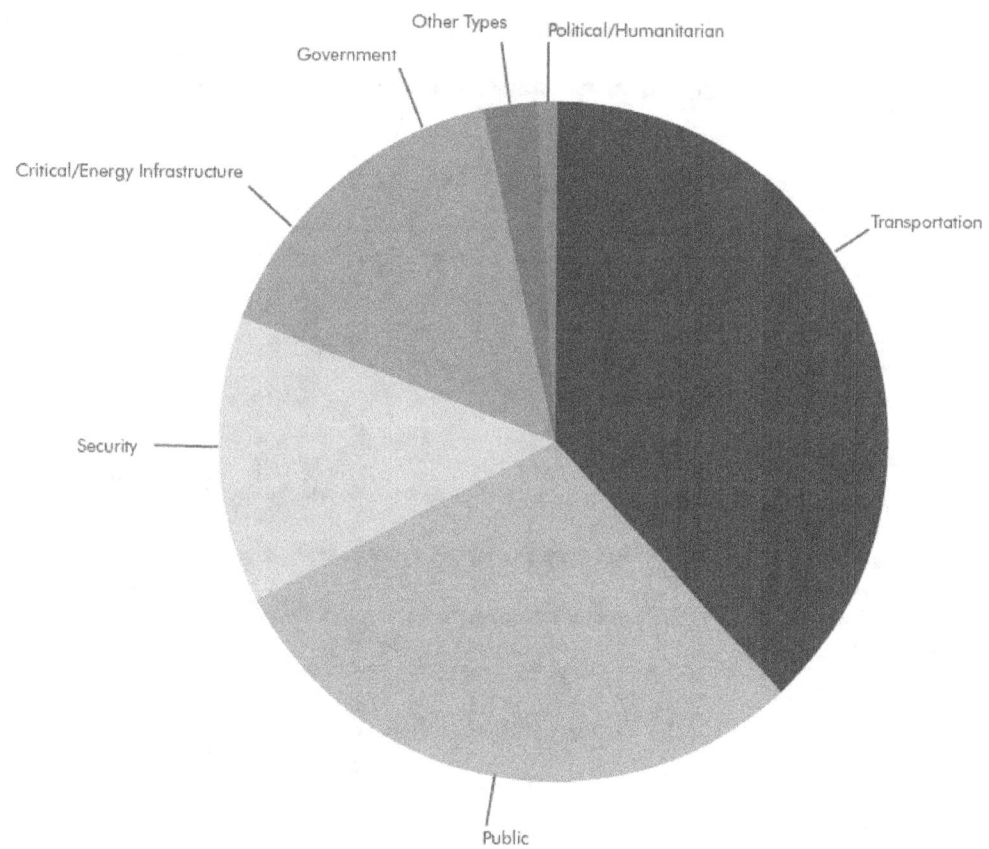

- Attacks on government facilities decreased by about 43 percent from 2010, from 796 attacks to 453 attacks in 2011.

Attacks on Energy Infrastructure
(2007-2011)

- There was a sharp increase in the number of attacks directed at energy infrastructure, including fuel tankers, fuel pipelines, and electrical networks, rising from 299 attacks in 2010 to 438 attacks in 2011.

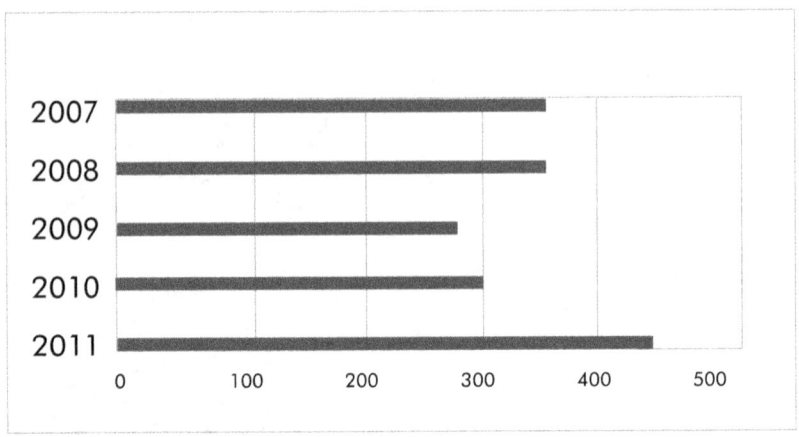

Attacks on Public Places
(2007-2011)

- The number of attacks directed at public places declined in each of the past five years, from a high of 4,121 attacks in 2007 to 2,186 attacks in 2011.

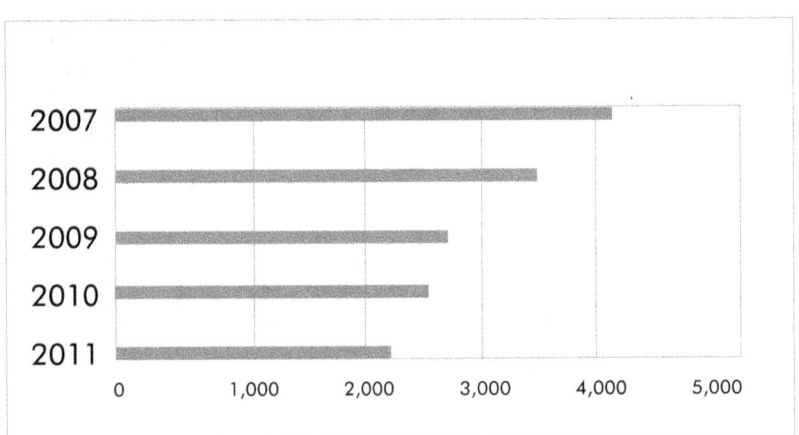

National Counterterrorism Center _____

U.S. Private Citizen Victims

S   eventeen U.S. private citizens worldwide were killed by terrorist attacks in 2011.[1] These deaths
    occurred in Afghanistan (15), Jerusalem (1), and Iraq (1). Overall, U.S. private citizen deaths
    constituted only 0.13 percent of the total number of deaths worldwide (12,533) caused by terrorism
in 2011. Fourteen U.S private citizens were wounded by terrorism in 2011; 10 in Afghanistan, three in
Jerusalem, and one in Iraq. Three U.S. private citizens were kidnapped in 2011; one in Pakistan, one in
Iraq (who was released in 2012), and one in Somalia (who was rescued in 2012).

Terrorism Deaths, Injuries, and Kidnappings of Private U.S. Citizens (2011)

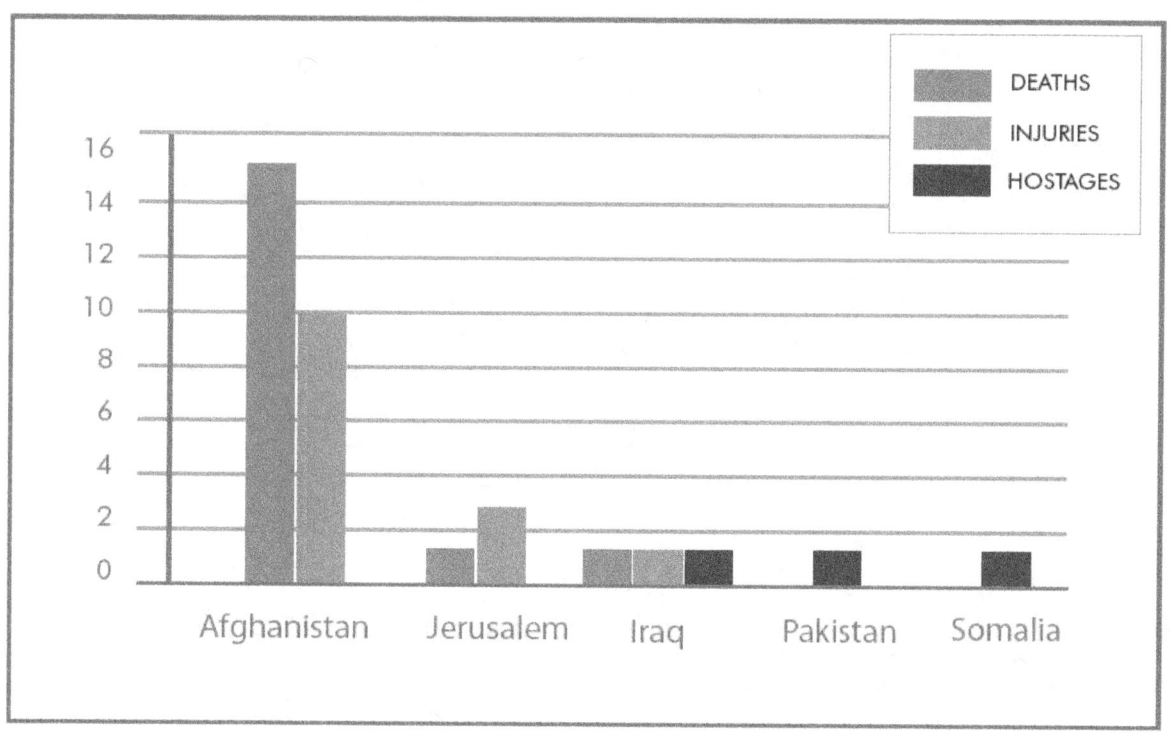

1 These numbers are provided by the U.S. Department of State, Bureau of Consular Affairs. The term "private U.S. citizen," refers to any U.S.
citizen not acting in an official capacity on behalf of the U.S. government. The cases enumerated reflect only those cases reported to, or known
by, the U.S. Department of State.

This page was intentionally left
BLANK

MONTHLY OVERVIEW

2011 Attacks that Resulted in Ten or More Fatalities

JANUARY

Government and Religious Sites Targeted; South Asian Markets Attacked

The bombing of an Egyptian church early on New Year's Day by the suspected group Army of Islam, began a month in which most of the mass-casualty terrorist attacks struck government facilities or officials or religious sites.

- Suspected Taliban in Kandahar, Afghanistan, killed a police commander in the bombing of a bathhouse.

- Tehrik-e-Taliban Pakistan (TTP) claimed responsibility for a VBIED attack against a police station.

- AQI claimed responsibility for a suicide vest and a VBIED attack against police and security forces, and was believed responsible for VBIED attacks against processions of Shia pilgrims during the holiday of Arba'een and at a Shia funeral.

- Attacks by al-Shabaab against the African Union Mission in Somalia (AMISOM) and Transitional Federal Government (TFG) troops caused dozens of civilians deaths.

- AQAP was the likely perpetrator of a complex attack in Yemen involving IEDs, rocket-propelled grenades (RPG), and small arms against a military convoy and government response vehicles.

Attackers also struck South Asian marketplaces and civilian vehicles with IEDs.

- The Taliban and Hizb-e-Islami claimed responsibility for a large-scale attack in Afghanistan in which a suicide bomber threw grenades and fired small arms into a supermarket before detonating an IED, killing multiple Filipino and Afghan civilians, several children, a government employee, and a humanitarian activist. Separately, an unclaimed IED attack killed 13 civilians and children.

- TTP claimed responsibility for a suicide bombing near a bazaar in Pakistan. Another separate IED attack inside a passenger bus killed and wounded dozens.

Major attacks also occurred in Russia and the Democratic Republic of the Congo.

- The Caucusus Emirate conducted a suicide bombing at the Domodedovo Airport in Russia, killing 37 civilians and wounding hundreds from a variety of different countries.

Domodedovo Airport, Russia

- In the Democratic Republic of the Congo, the Allied Democratic Forces (ADF) and the National Army for the Liberation of Uganda (NALU), believed to be working together, were suspected of kidnapping 15 civilians, 12 of whom were later killed.

FEBRUARY
Bombings Hit Crowds Near Government Institutions and Officials and Businesses

A spate of mass-casualty IED attacks occurred near government or security force buildings, checkpoints, and personnel.

- The Taliban claimed responsibility for a suicide IED attack at a government identity card facility in Afghanistan. In Iraq, suspected AQI carried out a suicide IED attack aboard a bus at a security checkpoint.

- VBIEDs were detonated at police stations in Afghanistan, Iraq, and Pakistan, killing dozens. A VBIED was detonated at a police training facility in Somalia, in which scores of trainees were killed or wounded.

- The deputy governor of al-Anbar, Iraq, was killed by a suicide bomber who detonated an IED at a Muslim celebration; several security officials and civilians were also killed.

Bombings targeted crowds at shopping and financial institutions.

- Taliban suicide bombers attacked the Kabul Bank in Jalalabad, Afghanistan, detonating an IED at the entrance and firing upon staff and customers inside. Separately, another Taliban suicide VBIED attack killed at least 10 people at a bazaar.

- Assailants in Iraq detonated a VBIED at an auto dealership, killing 13 civilians.

Numerous civilians died in mass-casualty fighting in Africa.

- Dozens of civilians and soldiers were killed in Somalia when al-Shabaab attacked AMISOM and TFG troops. In a separate incident, the Sool, Sanaag and Cayn (SSC) group attacked the Somaliland army, killing and wounding dozens of soldiers and civilians.

MARCH
Pakistan Suffers Uptick in Attacks; Lord's Resistance Army Conducts Kidnappings and Killings

Although Pakistan experienced only three mass-casualty attacks in January and one in February, the country suffered eight such attacks in March by militants in the Federally Administered Tribal Areas (FATA), Khyber Pakhtunkhwa province, and Balochistan.

- An IED carried by a suicide bomber was remotely detonated by other attackers near a compressed natural gas station and an office of Pakistan's Inter-Services Intelligence (ISI). Another suicide bombing killed dozens of tribal militants and civilians attending a funeral. TTP claimed responsibility for both attacks.

- The Baloch Liberation Front (BLF) claimed responsibility for firing onto a Frontier Works Organization camp in Balochistan Province, killing at least 11 government employees.

- Suicide bombers attacked two rallies of the Jamiat Ulema-e-Islam political party, killing dozens of civilians and several police officers.

- An IED attack at a mosque in Khyber Pakhtunkhwa province killed nine civilians and one child.

- Two small arms attacks against passenger vans in the FATA killed dozens. In one of the incidents, scores of people were kidnapped, at least 12 of whom were rescued by Pakistani security forces.

Several villages in the Central African Republic and the Democratic Republic of the Congo

MONTHLY OVERVIEW

were attacked by fighters probably affiliated with the Lord's Resistance Army (LRA). Dozens of civilians were killed and many were wounded or kidnapped.

Mass-casualty attacks continued apace in Afghanistan and Iraq, and one also occurred in Nigeria. Terrorist attacks in Somalia against AMISOM and Government forces resulted in large numbers of civilians killed.

- Probable Taliban operatives conducted IED attacks in Afghanistan against civilian vehicles, an army recruiting center, and a construction depot.

- A large-scale attack was launched at the Salah ad Din Provincial Council building in Iraq that involved mortars, VBIEDs, small arms, and a suicide attack. Scores of people were killed, including police officers, civilians, government employees, council members, and journalists. Nearly one hundred others were wounded, including several U.S. soldiers. Separately, after a suicide VBIED attack damaged a military building, several other IEDs were discovered nearby and rendered safe.

- A bomb thrown at a political rally of the ruling Nigerian People's Democratic Party killed 14. The government claimed that the opposition Congress for Progressive Change was responsible.

Al-Shabaab attacks against AMISOM and TFG troops killed dozens of civilians and soldiers. In one incident, al-Shabaab placed a VBIED that detonated prematurely when troops fired upon it. Separately, Somali University buildings were struck, leaving a professor and 14 others dead.

APRIL
Fewest Mass-Casualty Attacks During 2011

There were only 11 mass-casualty attacks in April, fewer than any other month in 2011.

- Unknown assailants in Morocco detonated two IEDs in a café, killing a waiter, a French child, and 15 civilians and wounding dozens more.

Marrakesh, Morrocco

- Pakistan suffered three mass-casualty attacks. In one attack claimed by TTP, two operatives wearing suicide vests struck a crowd at a Sufi Muslim shrine in Balochistan. A third operative was arrested before he was able to detonate his device. In another attack believed to be the work of the Taliban, an IED was detonated that killed 19 and destroyed a gambling club. In a third attack, Balochistan-based insurgents set fire to a bus, killing 15, including children.

- Two mass-casualty attacks occurred in Afghanistan. A suicide IED targeting an Afghan National Army bus killed seven soldiers and four civilians in Kabul, and a suicide bomber killed four tribal elders, two civilians, and five children in Kunar Province.

- In Iraq, there were two mass-casualty attacks. Suicide VBIEDs targeted official motorcades in Iraq's Green Zone, and an attacker with a suicide belt killed a dozen Shia worshippers at a mosque.

- A bomb killed or wounded dozens at Nigeria's Independent National Electoral Commission.

- Fifteen civilians were killed by an IED at a subway station in Belarus.

- A Somali public bus was destroyed in an IED attack, widely believed to be conducted by al-Shabaab, which killed or wounded two dozen civilians.

MAY

Complex Attacks Target Military and Police in Iraq, Nigeria, and Pakistan

Terrorists attacked a variety of military and police personnel and sites, incorporating multiple phases or tactics in unusually complex attacks.

- In Iraq, terrorists probably affiliated with AQI killed dozens of police officers in a coordinated attack. Assailants first detonated an IED attached by magnets to a vehicle near a police headquarters. Shortly thereafter, police investigating the scene were struck by a VBIED. When a police motorcade responded to the first explosions, it struck a roadside IED. Separately, assailants detonated a VBIED on a U.S. military patrol that wounded several soldiers. As Iraqi police arrived on the scene, a bomber detonated a suicide vest, killing or wounding dozens of police officers.

- In Nigeria, assailants probably affiliated with Boko Haram conducted a storming assault, firing small arms and throwing grenades into a police station, barracks, and bank.

- Militants believed to be TTP-affiliated carried out a large-scale attack at a naval base in Pakistan. The attackers destroyed aircraft with rocket-propelled grenades, detonated a

suicide vest, and fired upon military personnel with small arms. The attack left a dozen soldiers and several unknown victims dead and several aircraft damaged.

Terrorists used suicide vests or VBIEDs against several police and military targets, leaving many more dead or wounded.

- A suicide bomber in Afghanistan, for whom the Taliban claimed responsibility, detonated a VBIED near a bus carrying police cadets.

- A probable AQI suicide bomber in Iraq drove a VBIED into the entrance of a police headquarters building.

- Assailants probably from Boko Haram fired upon a police station and joint police and military patrol in Nigeria, prompting a battle which left multiple people dead or wounded.

- TTP claimed responsibility for a suicide IED attack against a Pakistan Frontier Constabulatory training center and two VBIED attacks targeting police stations.

Afghanistan and Pakistan-based militants also successfully targeted companies assisting with infrastructure and support in Afghanistan.

- Militants detonated an IED under a fuel tanker carrying supplies for NATO forces in Afghanistan, prompting multiple explosions that killed or wounded dozens.

- The Taliban was suspected in a small arms assault and an IED attack against road construction workers.

Mass-casualty attacks against crowds of civilians continued, including a VBIED attack at a market in Iraq, an attack with three nearly simultaneous IED explosions at a market in Nigeria, and several armed attacks in Somalia.

MONTHLY OVERVIEW

JUNE
Afghanistan and Yemen Experience Strategically Targeted Mass-Casualty Attacks

Terrorists in Afghanistan and Yemen conducted mass-casualty attacks against high-profile, strategic-level targets.

- Kabul's Intercontinental Hotel, a luxury hotel often frequented by foreigners, was attacked during a conference on the transition of security responsibilities from U.S. and NATO forces to Afghan control. The multi-hour assault was carried out by suicide bombers and assailants using small arms and RPGs. Eleven civilians and two police officers were killed, and more than a dozen others were wounded.

Kabul, Afghanistan

- In Yemen, militants probably from AQAP conducted a bombing at a mosque at the Presidential Palace. Then-Yemeni President Ali Abdallah Salih was badly wounded and several bodyguards and government officials were killed. Salih later departed the country for medical treatment and eventually left office after 33 years in power.

Complex attacks using a combination of tactics, secondary attacks against first responders, and simultaneous attacks all continued to be major sources of casualties.

- Indian extremists, probably from the CPI-Maoist, killed 10 police officers in a two-phased attack that included detonating an IED and then firing upon an explosive ordnance disposal vehicle that responded to the explosion.

- Terrorists in Iraq detonated two roadside IEDs and a VBIED at crowds surrounding markets and government offices. Another suicide bomber detonated a VBIED targeting responders near a hospital. Separately, an AQI-claimed suicide bomber detonated an IED inside a Sunni mosque; seconds later, assailants detonated a roadside IED outside.

- Militants probably from TTP fired upon a Pakistani police station before detonating suicide vests, killing or wounding dozens. The militants then separately assaulted a joint police and military checkpoint using small arms, RPGs, and mortars. The militants abducted and later killed 16 police officers captured during the raid. In another incident in Pakistan, a timed IED drew a crowd that was then attacked by a suicide bomber on a motorcycle.

Terrorists also conducted major attacks against a variety of high-profile and culturally significant or symbolic locations, factional opponents, and civilian gatherings.

- A suicide bomber in Afghanistan detonated a VBIED at a hospital and dozens of civilians were killed in three other IED attacks that included a minibus carrying a family and an outdoor market.

- A suicide bomber in Iraq detonated a VBIED at a checkpoint outside the late-Saddam Hussein's former presidential compound. In separate incidents, VBIEDs exploded outside a restaurant frequented by soldiers and police officers and near a provincial governor's home. Assailants also detonated three IEDs at a market and at a Shia mosque.

- Boko Haram claimed responsibility for an assault on a bar in Nigeria that killed 25 and wounded 30.

- Assailants from Afghanistan crossed into Pakistan and fired small arms and RPGs on three villages and a checkpoint, killing civilians, pro-Islamabad tribal militia, and paramilitary troops. Militants in this attack also kidnapped 20 tribal militia members. Separately, a suicide bomber detonated an IED inside an Army-run bakery in Pakistan.

- Al-Shabaab was widely believed to be responsible for a mortar attack that killed 13 Ugandan peacekeepers and a small arms assault on a camp affiliated with the Sufi pro-government Ablu Sumah wal Jama'a organization. Separately, tribal militants ambushed vehicles with a small arms attack, killing between nine and 11 people.

JULY
Large-Scale Attacks in Norway and India; Ten Mass-Casualty Attacks Hit Afghanistan

Mass-casualty attacks in Oslo, Norway, and Mumbai, India, received widespread media coverage and worldwide attention. The attack in Norway was the deadliest in that country since the Second World War, and the attack in India was reminiscent of the multi-day assault in late November 2008 by Lashkar-e-Tayyiba operatives.

- A lone wolf detonated a VBIED outside the office of the Norwegian Prime Minister and two hours later fired upon a political summer camp attended predominantly by young adolescents. In total, the attacker killed 33 children, 34 political affiliates and seven government employees in the assault.

Oslo, Norway

- Operatives probably from the Indian Mujahideen (IM) detonated three IEDs at two crowded market places and near a bus stop, killing dozens and wounding hundreds.

Afghanistan suffered a rash of mass-casualty attacks against NATO forces, workers supporting international and Afghan forces, and Afghan civilians.

- Several French and Afghan soldiers were killed when a suicide attacker detonated an IED near a NATO convoy.

- Seven suicide bombers and other assailants with IEDs, VBIEDs and small arms attacked the offices of the Uruzgan provincial governor, a local television station and the compound of a militia commander. Separately, a suicide bomber killed between 10 and 12 police officers and one child by detonating a VBIED outside a police headquarters.

- Armed assailants fired upon a convoy transporting supplies for NATO forces and on laborers constructing a police checkpoint.

- During two incidents in the same town, Taliban insurgents attacked police checkpoints and set fire to several houses.

- Other IED explosions against vehicles killed

MONTHLY OVERVIEW

or wounded dozens.

Complex attacks in Iraq continued to produce high casualty numbers.

- Assailants believed to be members of AQI detonated a VBIED in a parking lot and then targeted responders with a roadside IED.

- AQI attacked soldiers and police officers collecting their paychecks, first by detonating a VBIED at al-Rafidain bank then deploying a suicide bomber against responders. The incident left 16 soldiers, police officers, and civilians dead.

Militants in Pakistan, for whom Lashkar-i-Jhangvi (LJ) claimed responsibility, fired upon a van transporting Shia civilians, killing 11.

AUGUST

High-Profile Attacks Conducted on British Council in Afghanistan and the UN in Nigeria

The wave of mass-casualty attacks garnering extensive media attention in July continued into August with two major attacks on diplomatic institutions.

- The Taliban claimed responsibility for assailants who breached the gate of the British Council compound in Kabul with a with small arms and suicide vests. Seven civilians, five police officers, and a New Zealand soldier were killed and dozens more were wounded.

- Boko Haram claimed responsibility for a suicide bomber who crashed a VBIED into the lobby of a UN building in Abuja, Nigeria, and then detonated the explosives, killing dozens and wounding scores. This was the first Boko Haram attack against Western targets.

Abuja, Nigeria

Extremists in Iraq and Pakistan also conducted more mass-casualty attacks during this month against mosques than other months, due probably to the significance of attacking religious targets during Ramadan and the increased crowds that surround such targets.

- A suicide bomber in Iraq killed or wounded scores of people by detonating an IED at a Sunni mosque.

- TTP claimed responsibility for a suicide bomber who detonated a vest at a Pakistani mosque. Separately, probable Baloch or Sunni extremists detonated a VBIED at a mosque.

Terrorists in Afghanistan, India, Iraq, and Nigeria continued to conduct major assaults using large numbers of personnel and complex tactics.

- In an assault tactically similar to the British Council attack conducted one week prior, Taliban assailants used a VBIED to breach the gate of the Parwan governor's house and then launched small arms, RPGs, and two suicide bombings inside the building compound, killing 16 government employees and six police officers.

- In India, a group of over 100 armed assailants probably affiliated with the CPI-Maoist group fired upon several military or paramilitary patrols, killing a dozen people.

MONTHLY OVERVIEW

- Iraqi terrorists probably affiliated with AQI detonated an IED in a marketplace, then detonated a VBIED as first responders arrived.

- Boko Haram garnered widespread attention when it conducted a multi-target attack in which operatives aboard buses fired small arms and threw grenades at a local police headquarters before proceeding to and robbing the United Bank of Africa. Multiple police officers were killed as well as bank employees and customers.

Six other mass-casualty attacks against buses, hotels, police, and shopping areas also occurred in Afghanistan, Pakistan, and Somalia.

SEPTEMBER
Shia Pilgrims, Funerals Attacked in Iraq and Pakistan; Blast Hits New Delhi High Court

Terrorist attacks in Iraq and Pakistan caused the deaths of dozens of Shia pilgrims and funeral attendees.

- Probable AQI operatives set up a fake checkpoint in Al-Anbar Province, Iraq, ordered pilgrims aboard a bus traveling to Syria to disembark and then systematically executed them. Separately in Pakistan, LJ militants also stopped a bus transporting pilgrims to Iran, forced them to disembark and executed them.

- Assailants in Iraq detonated a VBIED at a Shia funeral, killing or wounding dozens.

Both Harakat ul-Jihad Islami (HUJI) and IM claimed responsibility for an IED attack in India outside the Delhi High Court that killed 15 civilians and wounded at least 91 others.

Three other mass-casualty attacks in Afghanistan, including an ambush of police officers approaching a residence, an attack on a construction company convoy, and the detonation of a roadside IED against a bus, resulted in the deaths of dozens of police officers, private security guards, and civilians.

Armed assailants probably from the group National Forces for Liberation (FNL) stormed the Chez les Amis bar in Burundi, killing the bar owner and 38 civilians.

Probable AQI members continued to use VBIEDs to attack crowds in Iraq.

- A VBIED detonated near a crowd outside a government office; minutes later, additional IEDs targeting first responders detonated, leaving at least 17 dead and over 100 wounded.

- Another VBIED killed 15 and wounded 46 in an attack on a restaurant.

Pakistani militants probably affiliated with TTP conducted a complex attack against the home of the Frontier Constabulatory Deputy Inspector General. A suicide bomber detonated a VBIED outside of the residence and then a suicide bomber entered the home, threw grenades and detonated an IED. Thirteen soldiers, 12 civilians and three children were killed in the attack. Separately, a suicide bomber from an unknown group detonated an IED at an outdoor funeral.

Dozens of civilians were killed by al-Shabaab attacks in Somalia where militants targeted TFG forces and members of the Ras Kamboni militia.

MONTHLY OVERVIEW

OCTOBER

Iraq Continues to Suffer Complex Attacks; Attacks Hit Military Bases in Afghanistan; Multiple Attacks Occur in Somalia

Complex IED attacks continued to be the primary tactic used in mass-casualty attacks in Iraq.

- Three separate incidents targeted crowds with an IED and responders with secondary IEDs detonated minutes later.
- Separately, eight police officers and six civilians were killed in a VBIED attack on a police station.

Afghanistan suffered two attacks against U.S. military bases which resulted in mass casualties.

- A suicide bomber detonated a VBIED against a military transport bus, killing multiple Coalition soldiers and several civilians.
- An IED magnetically attached to a tanker at Bagram Air Base detonated, causing a fuel leak; hours later, dozens of civilians scavenging for gasoline were killed or wounded in a secondary explosion.

Somalia also suffered a surge in mass-casualty attacks, most of which were directed at AMISOM and TFG forces but affected civilian targets.

- A landmine in a market killed 16 civilians.
- A suicide truck bomb against a government compound killed 100 civilians and children.
- A VBIED near a building housing several government ministries killed 10 to 15 civilians. Al-Shabaab was widely believed to be responsible, but denied responsibility.

Pakistani militants continued to target Shia Muslims; 14 were killed in a small arms attack on a bus.

NOVEMBER

Attacks Hit Burma and Senegal; Boko Haram Conducts Wave of Bombings

Burma suffered its only mass-casualty attack of the year in November and Senegal experienced its first.

- Terrorists on motorcycles threw a grenade into a Burmese orphanage, killing seven adults and three children and injuring dozens more.
- Assailants probably affiliated with the Movement of Democratic Forces of Casamance (MFDC) killed 10 Senegalese civilians.

Boko Haram claimed responsibility for an attack in which assailants fired upon and detonated IEDs and a VBIED near a bank, several police stations, and six churches.

Five IED attacks in Baghdad left scores dead.

- Three VBIEDs exploded near a group of coffee shops.
- A suicide bomber detonated an IED at a meeting of a Sons of Iraq council, and then targeted responders with a VBIED. In a separate complex attack, two IEDs targeted a market; a third detonated as responders arrived.
- Three IEDs hit a market area in Baghdad.
- A suicide bomber detonated a VBIED at the entrance to a prison, killing and wounding civilians, police officers, and government employees.

In Pakistan, a suicide bomber targeted a prison van, wounding 10 police officers.

Assailants in Afghanistan and Somalia killed scores in separate IED and small arms attacks.

- Assailants fired on a logistics convoy transporting supplies for NATO forces and detonated an IED near a convoy of private security contractors. Separately, a landmine in Afghanistan exploded near a police convoy.

- Al-Shabaab was most likely responsible for two IED attacks in Somalia.

DECEMBER
Boko Haram Conducts IED Attacks; Former Government Officials Targeted in India and Pakistan

Boko Haram claimed responsibility for three major IED attacks in Nigeria.

- Multiple IEDs detonated near several churches and a VBIED detonated at a State Security headquarters.

- Small arms attacks and IEDs targeted security forces, residences, buildings, a mosque, and several churches.

- A roadside IED killed or wounded many civilians, including children.

Government officials and their families were targeted in India and Pakistan.

- In India, militants probably from the CPI-Maoist group launched an IED and small arms attack on a convoy carrying a former state legislative speaker, killing 12 police officers and one civilian.

- The Balochistan Liberation Army claimed responsibility for a VBIED explosion outside the home of the son of a former state minister that killed nine civilians and seven bodyguards.

Afghanistan and Iraq each suffered four major IED attacks.

- Two suicide IED attacks targeted funerals in Afghanistan, one of which hit Shia mourners and was claimed by LJ. Separately, roadside IEDs hit a passenger bus and a police patrol.

- In Iraq, VBIEDs targeted shops and a suicide attack was directed at the Iraqi Integrity Commission. An AQI-claimed complex attack involving an IED and a suicide VBIED targeted construction workers. Separately, three IEDs struck Shia pilgrims.

Senegal, Somalia, and Syria each suffered one mass-casualty attack.

- Senegalese assailants, probably from the MFDC, fired RPGs on a military outpost and vehicle.

- Probable al-Shabaab-linked kidnappers killed 11 Somali civilians and assaulted and wounded many others.

- Two suspected AQI female suicide bombers detonated VBIEDs at Syrian intelligence facilities, killing or wounding scores of soldiers, civilians, and government employees.